WHAT EVERY STUDENT SHOULD KNOW ABOUT PRACTICING PEER REVIEW

Michelle Trim
Lander University

D0226456

PEARSON
Longman

New York   San Francisco   Boston
London   Toronto   Sydney   Tokyo   Singapore   Madrid
Mexico City   Munich   Paris   Cape Town   Hong Kong   Montreal

Director of Development: Mary Ellen Curley
Development Editor: Lai T. Moy
Executive Marketing Manager: Megan Galvin-Fak
Project Coordination, Text Design, and Electronic Page Makeup: WestWords, Inc.
Senior Designer: Sue Kinney
Cover Illustration: Veer Images
Senior Manufacturing Buyer: Alfred C. Dorsey
Printer and Binder: Courier Corporation
Cover Printer: Courier Corporation

Library of Congress Cataloging-in-Publication Data

Trim, Michelle.
  What every student should know about practicing peer review / Michelle Trim. -- 1st ed.
     p. cm.
  Includes bibliographical references and index.
  ISBN-13: 978-0-321-44848-4
  1. English language--Rhetoric--Study and teaching. 2. Report writing--Evaluation. 3. Col-
lege prose--Evaluation. 4. Peer review. I. Title. II. Title: Practicing peer review.
PE1404.T775 2006
808'.042071--dc22
                                   2006013070

Please visit us at www.ablongman.com

ISBN 0-321-44848-0

4 5 6 7 8 9 10—CRS—09 08 07

CONTENTS

INTRODUCTION

This text is intended for students who may be encountering peer review at the college level for the first time. Peer review is a process used by professionals outside the college setting and by students in college courses. In the corporate world, in research settings, and in information-rich workplace environments, peer review and team writing are often used to enhance the quality and effectiveness of written documents. These peer reviews can be conducted in person using traditional tools like pens and paper, on the computer using special peer review software or word processors, online using the Web to distribute drafts and responses, and online using peer review software that facilitates communication as well as the review itself.

Basically, peer review is a process by which peers read and respond to writing. The purpose of this process in an educational setting is typically twofold:

1. To aid student writers in improving the success of their drafts by "testing" them on fellow students who act as readers/reviewers and offer feedback
2. To learn more about the topic, research, and/or the writing process through conversation and the exchange of ideas between writers and readers

College teachers may assign peer review more than once as part of a writing assignment: once to help students generate ideas and then again to aid students in revising their drafts. A review may or may not take place during class time. Students are put into groups and then they exchange their written drafts. Teachers often supply students with a list of questions to guide their review of their classmates' written texts. After a student writes his/her responses to the questions, he/she may engage in conversation with the writer about the draft and the review. This part of the process is often regarded as crucial to the educational purpose of the review. Through these conversations, students often develop new ideas and gain new perspectives on their topics.

Sometimes peer review assignments are not as thoroughly explained as students might want them to be. Students may wish to provide quality feedback to their peers, but may not always feel like they know what to say. In this text, the sections on early draft and developed draft peer review seek to provide students with an understanding of how to answer some of the more commonly used peer review questions. The goal of these sections is not to attempt to provide an exhaustive list of all questions that students might use to examine a peer's text, but rather, for students to develop an understanding of what kind of feedback is most helpful to writers.

The section on electronic peer review describes some of the more common methods currently used to take advantage of electronic technology to conduct peer review. There are many ways to use these tools; this section of the text represents a desire to familiarize students with alternate ways of doing peer review. These methods might also be of interest to students who are not being asked to complete peer reviews in class. As more and more colleges become fully integrated with electronic technology, electronic peer review may begin to replace the conventional classroom, small group setting. Students may be expected to complete peer reviews online, outside of class or in class using a computer-based classroom. As technology advances, more ways of using it to improve writing will be developed. For now, this text hopes to supply students with some of the strategies used in electronic peer review that they can adapt as suits them best.

The sections on group dynamics aim to address some of the uncomfortable and difficult situations with group members that sometimes arise through the sharing of student work. These experiences can be avoided if readers and writers have a better understanding of where the boundaries lie between engaging with a person's writing and engaging with that person's beliefs and feelings. The communicative space during peer review when readers and writers discuss their drafts is precious to the development of strong writing skills. It is important that students develop good communication skills in talking to each other about writing so that peer review does not degenerate into a battle of attitudes or devolve into a simple editing session.

The sample student texts in the last section are included to provide examples of certain kinds of comments that are typical for peer review. These are not models nor are they intended to be ideal examples of the perfect way to do peer review. They are just samples of good practices that students might find useful in learning how to write comments for their peer review experiences. The sample drafts are short and therefore the comments are limited to a draft of that length. Readers should focus on the tone of the comments, the suggestions offered, and the kind of writing challenges the comments address. To illustrate the use of a typical feature in word processors, a revision of the developed draft sample is included. This revision was completed with the track changes feature turned on, as described in the electronic peer review section. Finally, a list of additional readings is offered for students who want to learn more about writing, working in groups, and peer review.

1
TRADITIONAL PEER REVIEW

What Is It?

Traditional peer review is a widely used part of the writing process that college students often experience in their first year composition courses. Writers use peer review at various times in their writing process to improve the quality of their revisions. It is called "peer" review because reviewers are typically peers of the writer. This holds true regardless of what level of writing is being reviewed. Professionals in a wide variety of fields use peer review as part of their ordinary practice. In academic professions, journal articles are often peer reviewed prior to publication. This means that professional writers often expect that their writing will be reviewed by other professionals with similar areas of expertise.

Most writers hope that peer review will provide them with necessary information about how their writing comes across to its readers. Having some idea of how readers receive a text helps writers develop their writing so that it best communicates what they are trying to say. Learning how to make one piece of writing more effective benefits writers because they can use what they learn about one draft to make the next draft that much better. The more a writer revises the text, the more the writer learns about what she is trying to say. The goal of developing good peer review skills is not to learn how to write perfect first drafts but to acquire the skills necessary to revise texts into more effective second and third drafts.

For students, this means that they read and review each others' writing. Through that process of reading and responding, students have the opportunity to see how someone else is trying to get his or her ideas across. By thinking about how to advise a writer to make his or her draft more effective, the reviewer learns something about what kind of writing works better than another.

The traditional practice of peer review has five main steps:

1. Identify peer review partners/participants
2. Exchange drafts to be reviewed
3. List items to be targeted in the review
4. Read drafts/comment
5. Exchange reviewed drafts

Peer review can occur at any stage of the drafting process, but most peer review practices fall into one of two categories:

1. Reviews of early drafts
2. Reviews of developed drafts

Peer Review of Early Drafts

What Is It?

Early drafts, also called invention drafts and discovery drafts, typically represent a writer's first stab at writing about an idea. These drafts may or may not have been carefully proofread. They are often a talking-through of the writer's ideas and may not reflect attention to audience, organization, and/or adequate explanation. What they do reflect is the writer's attempt to convert his or her thoughts and ideas into a written text. This conversion is an important part of the writing process. Ideas do not usually exist in people's minds in carefully organized formats like college essays. Therefore, writers face the challenge of capturing their ideas and transcribing them into a written format that makes sense to others. Like any complicated process, this requires several attempts to achieve the best results possible. Learning how to make each attempt more effective helps students develop strong writing skills that they carry with them even after an assignment is finished. Writers must get their ideas on paper before they can then revise them to take the shape of a college essay or any other professional written text. Peer review can be a useful tool for writers to get their ideas past that first stage to a more developed, more successful written text.

Common Practices

Once the writer has created a text that represents his or her first attempt at getting ideas on paper, that writer is ready to begin thinking about where she or he wants that text to go. The writer will need to determine the following to successfully revise this early draft:

1. Who is my audience?
2. What is the main idea I want to get across to my reader?
3. What information does my reader need to know about my idea for it to make sense?
4. Do I need examples?
5. Do I need evidence or support for any claims I am making?
6. Have I selected a topic that is appropriate to my writing task? Does it need to be more general? More focused?
7. Are my points organized in a logical way?

These questions are the kind of "big picture" questions a reviewer might try to answer to help the writer develop his/her early draft. Some of these questions might be revisited in a later stage of peer review as ideas get shuffled around and reorganized. Writers should expect responses to these questions to drive a significant re-working of their text. First drafts are called rough drafts for a reason. Writers need to be prepared to completely revise their first drafts after a successful peer review session, because one of the goals of the review is to help writers develop their ideas. Here is a more detailed explanation of each question.

1. Who is the audience?

Audience refers to both the intended and unintended readers of your text. In other words, an essay for a course has an intended audience of the teacher, but it might also have an expected, but unintended, audience of other members of the class. Successful writers target specific audiences to make their writing fit with what the reader can understand while making their point as effectively as possible. Some assignments ask students to imagine audiences other than the instructor. In these cases, students need to match language usage, tone, amount of explanation, and type of writing to that which will be most effective for their assigned audience.

For example, an assignment might ask a student to write a letter to an elected official, such as a member of Congress or a city mayor, that makes a specific argument for something that the writer wants the official to do. The student needs to construct her text so that it makes the reader want to listen to what she has to say. If the writer uses informal language or doesn't get to the point quickly enough, someone as important as an elected official might stop reading or worse, take offense.

Writing that targets a specific audience is always more successful in communicating ideas to that audience. Reviewers should try to think about what audience is targeted by the text and offer suggestions for ways that the writer might alter the organization of ideas, language, or overall tone to best fit that audience.

2. What is the main idea?

Successful student papers usually have a clearly stated, central organizing idea. One way to think of this is to compare a student essay to a house. The foundation of a house determines its shape as well as its height. A weak foundation will cause the house to fall down or sag in places, making it distorted and strange. The main idea of a text works the same way. If it is not clear to the reader, then the shape of the paper will seem vague and hard to figure out. If the idea is too small to support the length of the paper, then it will seem to flounder like an unsteady wall. Likewise, if the main idea is too large, it may seem unfinished and underdeveloped like a one-story house on a two-story foundation.

The first thing a reviewer should do in answering a question like this is to identify what he thinks is the main idea in the draft. If that does not match what the writer intended, this information alone is valuable to the writer. In a face-to-face peer review, the reviewer can communicate this to the writer to determine what other information the reviewer can provide about the main idea. Once the main idea is identified, the reviewer should consider the topic sentences of the subsequent paragraphs to determine if they seem to support the main idea identified or if they do not seem to fit.

3. **What information does the reader need to know about an idea for it to make sense?**

   In many ways this question is about understanding the audience of a text. Deciding how much information is enough requires the writer to have some idea of what the reader knows about the topic. To answer this question usefully for the writer, both reviewer and writer need to be in agreement as to who constitutes the audience for the draft. An educated audience can handle more complex ideas and more specific vocabulary, but no amount of general education can prepare a reader for jargon that is outside of his experience. For example, let's say that for his psychology class, a student wanted to write a paper about the history of anti-depressant prescription medication. The instructor may or may not have specific training in biochemistry or pharmaceutical drugs. To be safe, writers should err on the side of caution and explain any drug or medical terminology that they decide to use in their writing. Without this explanation, the reader might not be able to adequately access the ideas that the writer is trying to get across. A good reviewer helps the writer by pointing out language and concepts that they do not understand.

4. **Are examples needed?**

   Answering this question depends on how well the reader understands what the writer is trying to say. If the reader is unclear as to what point or points a writer is trying to make, then more examples that provide detailed explanation are probably needed. Once the reviewer communicates problem spots to the writer, the writer can decide if the lack of understanding can best be solved through the use of examples or if there is another solution. The best course of action on the part of the reviewer is to point out every place where the main idea or supporting ideas are unclear. That way, the writer has enough information to decide how best to address the problem.

5. **Is evidence or support needed?**

   A general rule of thumb says that any fact that is not common knowledge needs to be supported by some kind of external evidence that can be cited. Some claims cannot be proved no matter how much evidence is collected. For example, it is impossible to prove that all young people like alternative music. It is highly unlikely that any researcher could have access to every young person in order to prove this point. The job of the reviewer is to help the writer determine which claims need to be supported with evidence and which claims simply need to be revised. A writer could probably find evidence to support a claim that states that "Many young people prefer alternative music to other musical styles."

Having adequate support lends credibility to the writer. If a writer is not credible, then he will have a difficult time communicating his ideas convincingly to the reader. By helping the writer locate areas of the text that need support or revision to function effectively, the reader will develop a similar sensitivity in her own writing. Good reviewers look for:

- Sweeping generalizations (All women are . . . People everywhere agree . . . Everyone knows . . .)
- Unsupported claims that look like facts (Dogs are more violent than cats; Children who read a lot of books do better in school; Crop circles are caused by silent thunderstorms)
- Facts that may not be common knowledge (Children can overdose on vitamins; Solar energy can be expensive to harness; Red wine has positive health benefits)

Getting feedback early in the writing process on what items need more support can help the writer plan what additional research is needed.

6. **Is the topic appropriate to the writing task? Does it need to be more general? More focused?**

To answer this question, the reviewer needs to be familiar with the assignment. First, the reviewer should look over the assignment and make sure that the writer's draft matches what the teacher has assigned. Lack of development is usually indicated by an overly short text that does not adequately explain all of its points. By looking over the answers to the previous five questions, the reviewer should be able to communicate what areas of the paper need more development. But, length alone should not be used to answer this question. An early draft is by definition in process, and as such is unfinished. If the paper lacks specific information, then that is a reason to suggest to the writer that she needs more explanation, examples, or a narrower topic that can be explored with greater detail.

7. Are the main points of the draft organized in a logical way?

There are many good ways of going about answering this question for a writer. One way asks reviewers to circle the writer's main point and the topic sentence of each paragraph. After these points are circled, then the reviewer should look at them to see if they seem to occur in a logical order and if the topic sentences fit with the main point of the draft. If the writer is using complex terminology, for example, then the use of those terms should be defined early in the draft rather than later. A good reviewer has two goals in answering this question. First, she needs to identify how the draft is organized from a reader's perspective. Second, the reviewer needs to let the writer know if his method of organization works or if there might be a better way to organize the main points. Some examples of ways to organize a draft include:

1. Moving from least important to most important
2. Chronological order
3. Order of a process (if it is a process draft, meaning a how-to paper, then the ideas need to follow the order of the process—step one, then step two, etc.)

Answering these questions requires more space than the margins of a student paper provide. Although it is always helpful to connect a comment to the specific paragraph or sentence to which it refers, there just isn't enough room to adequately explain some responses in small spaces. Reviewers should get in the habit of developing some kind of means of referencing the pieces of a text that they are commenting about. An easy way to do this is to simply number the sentences in each paragraph and then number each paragraph. That way, a reviewer can clearly indicate, for example, that "sentence four in paragraph three" needs more support or explanation. Thoughtful, narrative comments that are specific in nature make the most useful feedback for writers. Reviewers should avoid general language that does not communicate much that the writer can use. For example, telling a writer that a paper is "nice," or that "the topic seems interesting," sounds friendly, but doesn't provide guidance as to how the writer can improve her text. Questions like those discussed previously are intended to help reviewers develop their responses so that they don't feel "stuck" when trying to figure out what to say.

Reviewers are often instructed to write comments on the drafts they are reviewing. While longer, more thoughtful comments are usually better for an early draft stage, over-commenting on details of language and writing style can be confusing and counterproductive. See Sample #1 in the Additional Resources section. Notice how items are boxed and underlined with comments connected to them. Is it clear what piece of feedback is most important? Notice that several comments relate to the phrasing of sentences and language use. For an early draft peer review, these comments are not as helpful because the language will most likely significantly change when the writer makes his next revision. Figuring out how to organize the ideas needs to happen before the writer makes sure that the words chosen best communicate those ideas.

Purposes

The primary purpose of peer review is usually to help writers improve the effectiveness of their writing by having it "test driven" by a peer. In professional contexts, peer reviews are often conducted to try to help the writer identify areas of her argument or research that have gaps so that the writer can go back and revise her paper with the new knowledge provided by the reviewer. Peer review in college-level courses works much the same way, except it offers an added benefit for the reviewer because both writer and reviewer are usually working toward the same writing goal.

Student writers are usually still developing their writing for academic audiences. As students approach completion of their academic studies, those audiences become more discipline specific. One of the best ways to learn how to write well for an academic audience is to read others' academic writing. When students engage in peer review, it is not just to help the writer; it helps both writer and reviewer at the same time because both are learning how to make writing for a specific writing task more effective. In discovering suggestions for how a peer review partner might improve her method of organization in a text, the reviewer discovers other ways that he might organize his text.

The other aspect of writing that students do not always recognize is that it is a method of learning just like reading. Most students are familiar with the idea that reading chapters in a textbook helps them learn new material. But, many are not aware that writing about a new subject, thinking through ideas and synthesizing information from outside sources into a writing assignment, also helps them learn new things. In providing another perspective through peer review, reviewers' comments can help writers think about their drafts in new ways. As writers write to take those comments into account, they discover new ways of thinking about and writing about their topics. This experience has the potential to teach both writers and reviewers new things about their topics and about writing.

Advantages and Disadvantages

Conducting peer reviews of early drafts provides both readers and writers with opportunities to get feedback on their writing when it is still early enough in the writing process to fully integrate that feedback into their revisions. By conducting these reviews in person, reviewers can ask questions and provide explanation of their comments at the time of the review.

If the reviewers have been instructed to provide comments in the margins of the writer's text, these comments can be difficult to read and absorb. It is always challenging to read another person's handwriting. In person, pen-and-paper peer review sessions can put the reviewer at a disadvantage for the following reasons:

1. Time is usually limited to one class period or there is more than one draft to read in a short span of time.
2. Comments and responses have to be written by hand. This takes time to do and makes changing/revising comments difficult to do neatly.
3. Handwriting can be difficult to interpret and takes up a large amount of space on the page.

These disadvantages usually do not outweigh the advantages some people find in being able to discuss a review with the reviewer after it has taken place. Many writers appreciate having the opportunity to ask a reviewer specific questions about the comments and suggestions. Those conversations often spark new ideas and aid the writer in taking her ideas in new directions.

Peer Review of Developed Drafts

What Is It?

A developed draft is one that has been through at least one stage of revision and/or peer review. Typically, students might think that they revise as they compose their drafts on the computer. This kind of "fixing" is really more like editing than true revision. *Revision*, as English teachers typically define it, is a process by which the writer takes another look at his or her writing in order to rethink what he or she is trying to communicate. The best revisions occur when a writer has been exposed to new information. This can happen when a writer participates in peer review and gains another perspective on a topic and/or when a writer encounters additional research or outside information related to the main ideas in his or her draft.

Once a draft is developed to a more complete state, it is ready to be reviewed in a closer, more detailed way. This kind of peer review happens later in the writing process and does not typically result in a significant reworking of the writer's draft. This kind of fine-grained analysis should not be confused with proofreading. Reviewers of developed drafts are typically instructed to not offer corrections for grammar or spelling errors.

Common Practices

As with peer review of early drafts, reviewers should have a set of questions that they seek to address through their reviews. Some of these questions may seem similar to those from earlier peer review experiences. This is because the reviewer has a slightly different goal in reviewing a developed draft and can answer an earlier question in a different way. For this kind of peer review, students should not expect help generating new ideas so much as refining the main points they wish to emphasize in their drafts. Here are some good questions for reviewers of developed drafts to consider:

1. What is the author's thesis or central organizing idea?
2. If it is a persuasive paper, what claims is the author making?
3. Is there adequate support?
4. Is source material correctly cited and integrated into the draft?

5. Do some areas of the draft need more explanation and/or definition?

6. Does the writer's language flow or do some areas seem difficult to understand?

7. Does the tone of the draft match the assignment and/or audience?

In answering these questions, reviewers need to be very specific. It is not enough to tell a writer that there are areas of a paper that are confusing. The reader must point out exactly which parts of the text do not make sense. This can be done in a number of ways (e.g., by circling every word or phrase that seems unclear). The key is to use one consistent method of notation. Sometimes teachers will provide students with instructions as to how all class members are to note problem areas of their review partner's drafts. If no instructions are given about ways to make notations, then the reviewer and writer should come to an agreement as to how each will make notations on the other's draft. Circling every unclear word or phrase is only helpful if the writer knows what the circles mean. A more detailed explanation of each question follows.

1. What is the author's thesis or central organizing idea?

The thesis or central organizing idea is the main point that the author is making in his draft. The thesis is usually comprised of one or two sentences that occur fairly early in the draft, often in the first paragraph. The best way to answer this question is by rephrasing the author's thesis into the reviewer's own words. This accomplishes two things for the writer. First, it lets the writer know if the main idea of the draft from the reader's point of view matches what the author intended. Second, it lets the writer know if the main idea makes sense to the reader.

If a writer discovers that her thesis is weak or unclear, then the overall effectiveness of the draft is likely in jeopardy. As mentioned in the previous section, the main idea of a draft is like the foundation of a house. If that foundation is not adequate to the task of supporting the building, then the building will fall down. If a thesis is not clear to the reader or if the reader's understanding of the thesis does not match what the writer intends, then the writer's overall message for the paper could be lost. At worst, the draft could fail completely if a weak thesis causes it to seem unfocused and disorganized. Readers like to know where writers are taking them and may give up on a text that does not adequately explain the writer's main point.

2. If it is a persuasive paper, what claims is the author making?

Before a reviewer can evaluate a text to see if it needs more support for its ideas, he must identify the claims being made in the draft. A claim is a statement that argues something. Examples of claims are "Cats are harder to train than dogs" and "Baseball is more difficult to master than golf." An argument or persuasive paper will have at least one central claim that it is trying to prove, but all texts typically have smaller claims in them. Every time there is a claim, the author has to decide if she needs specific support for that claim in order for her text to be credible. Statements of fact only require specific support if they are not common knowledge.

In answering this question, reviewers should simply identify any claims that they see in the writer's draft. The next question asks reviewers to evaluate the claims to see if they need additional support.

3. Is there adequate support?

Because the claims in the draft have already been identified, evaluating them for adequate support should not be too difficult. Reviewers need to ask themselves if the claim being made by the writer has enough support for it to be credible. Credibility does not require that the reader agree with the points being made by the writer, it just means that the writer has provided sufficient support for his claims to be plausible.

This support can take shape in a couple of different ways, the most obvious being outside evidence such as quotations or facts from documented outside sources. The other way the writer can provide support is through logical deduction and explanation. If a writer is writing from personal experience, for example, support takes shape in examples that further explain the author's claims.

Let's say an author was writing an essay about the importance of family vacations. If the author's main idea is that "Family vacations are important for healthy family relationships," then the author is also likely making several smaller claims that support this main idea. One of these might be that "Family members who spend time together away from home often develop closer relationships that result in fewer arguments once the vacation is over." The author can support this claim with examples of family members spending time together away from home and then presenting his perception of harmony or discord among family members both before and after the vacation takes place. This kind of support is adequate for this example and does not need to take the shape of quotations from expert texts on families. Without these additional examples, the writer's claim would not be supported and readers might not be convinced of the writer's credibility. Good reviewers let writers know if more research or examples are needed for the author to adequately support his claims.

4. **Is source material correctly cited and integrated into the draft?**

One of the more difficult writing skills to master has to do with appropriately integrating facts and examples from outside source material into a written text. Reviewers can help writers by first locating any "orphan" quotations that are not connected to sentences. Quotations cannot stand alone as self-explanatory points. They need to be introduced and explained if the reader is going to understand how the writer thinks the information contained in the quotations supports the ideas in the draft. Writers cannot assume that readers will see the same relationships between quoted material and the associated text.

After locating any quotations that need to be better connected to the text, reviewers can then evaluate how source information has been referenced to see if it matches the points it is there to support. A quotation indicating that there was an increase in car sales for the month of April does not automatically support a claim that Americans are borrowing more money than ever before. Good reviewers will inform writers of source material that needs to be explained, better integrated, and/or re-thought altogether.

5. **Do some areas of the draft need more explanation and/or definition?**

The best way to answer this question is for the reviewer to read the draft normally and mark any places that cause him or her to feel unsure or confused about what the author is trying to say. Next, the reviewer should go back to the places marked and try to determine if the writer can eliminate confusion through more examples or explanation. Good reviewers will point out terminology they do not understand so that the writer will know she needs to work on adding more definitions of terms.

It is key that the reviewer feel confident that his difficulty with the writer's text is a valid response. The reviewer should never worry that it is their lack of specific knowledge of a topic that causes confusion. It is the writer's job to evaluate the feedback offered by the reader to determine if their text assumes too much about the reader's knowledge. It is the reviewer's job to communicate those places of incomprehension so that the writer can make the determination of what to do. Oftentimes, a lack of adequate explanation or definition is accidental. When writers feel knowledgeable about a specific topic, they sometimes forget that their readers may not share their level of familiarity with the subject of the text.

6. Does the writer's language flow or do some areas seem difficult to understand?

Sometimes the best way to answer this question is for the reviewer to read the writer's draft aloud. If peer review situations do not permit this, then the next best thing is for the reviewer to read the draft with a pencil in hand, marking any places that seem awkward. When finished reading, the reviewer can then go back to those marks and decide if the problem has to do with clunky word combinations or grammatical errors. It is important to remember that peer reviewers are usually not grammar experts and therefore should not attempt to correct another student's grammatical mistakes. A better approach is for reviewers to simply point out the awkward passages to writers and communicate if the problem is with usage or if the reviewer thinks there might be a grammar problem that needs to be addressed. It is the writer's job to determine how he can best correct these problems.

7. Does the tone of the draft match the assignment and/or audience?

As with the previous question, the goal here is for the reviewer to point out passages or words in the text that do not seem to fit the writing task. For example, a formal essay should probably not contain slang or other kinds of casual language. Expressions that might be acceptable in everyday speech are often too informal for college writing assignments. Students should always be sure to refer to their assignments and ask their instructors about the intended audience for their texts.

Audience determines the level of written language that should be employed. An argument paper, for example, should not seek to antagonize its reader. A text that seeks to persuade cannot succeed if it alienates its intended audience. It is easy for some writers to become passionate about their subjects and to get carried away with the expression of that passion in their writing. It is always a good idea to try to help a writer see how he or she might not be achieving the balanced, academic tone expected of some college-level writing assignments.

Going along with tone is the voice implied through the use of pronouns in a text. Students often overuse *you, our, we,* and *I* in essays they write for classes. Some instructors will prohibit the use of some pronouns for this reason. Regardless of whether a teacher has stated a rule about this, the voice of the text needs to match its rhetorical purpose. For example, if a student were writing an essay on her summer vacation, it would make sense for her to use *I,* because she is writing about her personal experiences. On the other hand, a research paper about global warming should probably not contain *I* or *you.* Good reviewers will point out excessive or inappropriate pronoun use.

Once a reviewer has responded to questions like these, the writer will be able to revise his text into a more complete document. Because writing is always in process, texts can always be revised into new and often better pieces of writing.

Every writing situation is different. If peer feedback indicates that an idea is unworkable, then it is the writer's job to rework that idea to fit the assignment. Likewise, if a student knows that she struggles with certain grammatical and stylistic issues in writing, it is her responsibility, and not that of the peer reviewer, to solve this kind of writing challenge. Students should talk to their instructors about what resources are available to them on campus.

Purposes

Peer review of developed drafts helps writers achieve a more thoughtful version of their texts. The more developed the draft before peer review, the more helpful the responses will be. After writers use their peer reviewers' responses to revise, writers often get help proofreading their revised texts before they have to be turned in. This process results in more polished pieces of writing that have a much better chance of effectively communicating the intended message.

The process of reviewing developed drafts does not just benefit the writer. Reviewers see ways that their peers are organizing their ideas, citing sources, making arguments, and expressing opinions. As readers, reviewers see firsthand why using *you* over and over again gets confusing. After all, who is the *you* referring to? Reviewers also see why quotations that are left unattached to surrounding sentences seem not to be incorporated into the author's points. In working to offer possible solutions to these writing problems, reviewers develop strategies that they can take back to their own writing tasks. Over time, both as writers and reviewers, students develop a palette of writing tools that they can utilize to create successful pieces of writing, in school and in the workplace.

Advantages and Disadvantages

The kind of fine-grained analysis sought in the review of a developed draft is time consuming. Students engaging in this kind of peer review may find that they require significant time outside of class to complete their reviews. If students feel rushed, they may not provide the same quality of response as they would if they had adequate time to complete the task.

In addition, if student writers do not provide fully developed drafts for the peer review session, the reviewers may be severely limited in their ability to provide useful feedback. It is impossible to comment on the need for support in a paper if it is only half finished, for example. Likewise, a reviewer cannot evaluate the writer's use of source material if the writer has not done any research yet. Successful peer review of developed drafts requires time and commitment.

If done well, this kind of peer review offers wonderful benefits to both writers and reviewers that cannot be duplicated through any other kind of writing exercise. Being able to see how other student writers cope with similar writing tasks helps students develop different ways of approaching writing assignments. Having a fellow student see a draft in process can be less intimidating than giving it to an instructor.

Group Dynamics in Traditional Peer Review Situations

What Is It?

Peer review can occur between just two students or it can occur in groups of any size. The most common configuration is two or three students in a group in which each group member responds to each member's writing. But, peer review can also occur in a round-robin style with the entire class as one large peer group. Peer review groups may be chosen at random by the instructor, may be specifically chosen by the instructor, or may be chosen by students. Groups are often given instructions as to how to review each others' writing assignments, but may not always be provided with guidelines for how to conduct the peer review process. This section aims to provide some guidelines for students who want to know more about selecting peer review partners or group members, strategies for talking to other students about their writing, and how to cope with content that is difficult to encounter.

How to Select Peer Reviewers

A general rule of thumb for selecting peer reviewers says that friends do not always make the best peer review partners. It makes sense that a good peer reviewer is someone who can be honest in giving feedback to fellow student writers. A review that is not honest just isn't helpful. But, what does it mean to give an honest review?

The three Cs of good reviews are:

1. Critical
2. Constructive
3. Considerate

Although friends and dating partners are probably pretty good at being considerate, they might find it difficult to be critical in their reviews. It is hard to tell someone whose opinion matters a great deal that their facts are unsupported or that their thesis is weak or that they need to reorganize their ideas in order for them to make sense. On the other hand, friends may see being considerate as their primary task. They are responding to the writing of a friend, after all, and do not want to hurt their friend's feelings. That desire to be considerate can actually blind a reviewer to some of the problems in the writer's text that need help. Instead of offering constructive advice, the friend says nothing or that everything seems "fine."

So, the bottom line in selecting peer review partners is to look for students who can perform the three Cs, are dependable, and are thoughtful. In this case, trying to get the "smart" student in your group is less advisable than trying to find a sincere and reliable student. If reviews extend outside of class, the best peer groups will be those whose members feel responsible for completing the peer review, even if it infringes on their TV time.

Things to Remember About Responding to Others' Writing

Writing can sometimes be quite personal to the writer. Many writers feel attached to the content of their texts and may feel hurt if their text is not well received. In addition, writing often reflects a writer's thoughts and opinions about issues that she might not be ready to question. The reviewer's role is to help the writer get her point across in the most effective way possible. The reviewer's role is not to agree or disagree with the writer, convert the writer to any particular viewpoint, or argue with the writer about points in the text. Good reviewers learn to separate their opinions and feelings about the writer's topic from the points that the writer is attempting to make. The old adage that the world would be a boring place if everyone thought alike is true. When responding to a writer's text, the reviewer needs to always show respect for that writer's ideas. Remember, reviewers are to comment on the writing, not the writer.

In constructing comments, reviewers need to think about how easily what they are saying will be understood. Comments need to be specific and they need to target one thing at a time. Imagining oneself in the place of the writer might be helpful in deciding how much to say and when to say it. Typos and other obvious surface errors should not be the focus of any peer review. A reviewer might offer to help a writer proofread his or her next revision, but should not take time away from his response to edit a student's paper.

It is also a good idea to not cover the paper with so many lines, circles, and comments that it becomes a map of responses that is impossible to navigate. See the first sample draft at the end of this book for an example of such a review. First, notice the number of different marks on the page. There are underlines, squares, and written comments. Getting a paper like this back must feel a bit overwhelming at first. For writers to successfully absorb all the comments a reviewer must make, these comments need to be clear and easy to follow. Rather than filling up the margins, reviewers can write their responses on another sheet. Or, reviewers might decide that one kind of comment, such as that on the author's system of organization, needs to occur in the margins to be most effective; the rest of the response can be written on a separate sheet of paper.

Negotiating Difficult Content

Some students are surprised by some of the ideas they encounter in their classmates' writing. Certain topics, especially those that tend to be rather provocative in political arenas, can inspire passionate debate. When reviewers are asked to comment on text that contains attitudes and opinions that are very different from their own, they can sometimes feel uncomfortable responding. Students must remember to focus on the writing and the way the author expresses his ideas, not on the author or on ways the author's beliefs differ. Part of the benefit of peer review is that students will be exposed to new ideas. It is not necessary for students to agree on a particular point to be able to provide each other with useful feedback.

Encountering material that puts individuals outside of their comfort zones is part of living in the world today. Every issue has many sides, and it is essential that reviewers do not react to ideas that they find objectionable. If a reviewer encounters something that he believes crosses the line from different to hateful, then he should speak to his instructor. The challenge of encountering alternate views can be exacerbated by students who write in ways that display insensitivity to the beliefs of others. As mentioned in the section on traditional peer review, the audience must be the determining factor in choosing the tone and language used in a piece of writing. If writing is to be visible to others in a class, then it is essentially public writing.

Writing for a public audience requires authors to be sensitive in their treatment of subjects that some students might find offensive. The rights of writers and readers to express themselves must be equally balanced. A writer is entitled to her opinion on a given issue, but she must consider the feelings of classmates and teachers when composing texts that address sensitive or controversial subjects. This does not mean that all ideas are ok to write about for a college course or that a writer must sacrifice her opinions. Students who consciously seek to not cause hurt feelings and who genuinely respect others will usually not create a text that is a problem. In contrast, negative and harmful attitudes about race, gender, ethnicity, religion, and other similar subjects have no place in a student paper that will be read by another student or by a teacher.

2

ELECTRONIC PEER REVIEW

What Is It?

Regardless of what kind of technology a writer uses for peer review, the basic criteria for reviewing a draft is the same as that for traditional reviews using pen and paper. What electronic peer review offers most students is the ability to extend peer review outside of the classroom without sacrificing the thoughtful input of other students. This changes the dynamics of the peer review situation in ways that often impact the kinds of comments students make, when they comment, and where in the draft they locate their comments. Some students find it easier to compose their comments on the computer instead of handwriting responses in margins. Typewritten comments are easier to read and may take up less physical space, thereby allowing the reviewer to say more without feeling as if they might be running out of room to write. Typed comments can also facilitate the revision process by providing suggestions and comments inside the electronic draft. Rather than switching between several sheets of comments and marks, students may be able to see all peer review comments inside the electronic file containing their original draft.

There are three basic types of electronic peer review:

1. Tracking changes and commenting via word processing programs
2. Distributing comments via a discussion board or class e-mail list
3. Using specifically designed peer review software that is often Web-based

Peer Review Using Word Processing Software

What Is It?

The two primary methods for using word processing software, like Microsoft Word, for peer review are tracking changes and inserting comments. Track Changes is a function available in most word processing programs. It enables a reviewer to make changes, add comments, and suggest alternate formatting without permanently altering the original author's text. When a reviewer uses this feature to change a word, for example, she will first delete the word and then type in a replacement. But, with the tracked changes function enabled, nothing actually gets deleted. Instead, the unwanted word is marked with a line through it and the suggested replacement is underlined or displayed in a different color. The comment feature can be used independent of tracking changes because most word processors also enable users to insert comments into the text. Comments can appear in the margins with brackets or lines pointing to specific portions of the text or they can appear as pop-up bubbles when a reader hovers his mouse over portions of the text with inserted comments.

Common Practices

Students wishing to use the word processing method of peer review often begin by exchanging Microsoft Word or other word-processed files containing their drafts. This can be done a variety of ways, including posting the files on a discussion board or through Blackboard. Next, if the reviewer is working with a Word file, she opens her peer review partner's file and selects "Track Changes" under the "Tools" tab. Once this feature is enabled, additions and comments are usually indicated in red and comments become embedded captions or highlighted passages with floating comment boxes. All of the "tracked changes" are saved when the reviewer saves the file.

The comment function enables reviewers to attach feedback to a specific word, phrase, sentence, or paragraph. This makes it easier and less time consuming for reviewers to offer specific feedback by not having to explain to what text the comments refer. In some versions, comments can be inserted in Word by highlighting the text that you want to comment on and then clicking on the "Insert" tab and selecting "Insert Comment." This feature is an excellent way to respond to specific peer review questions like those concerning the thesis sentence, transitions, method of organization, and topic sentences. These elements of a paper are commonly evaluated in college English essays.

Sometimes it can be difficult for a writer to understand exactly what a reviewer found to be problematic about a draft. The "big picture" comments mentioned in the section on early draft peer review do not point out specific words, phrases, or sentences that need revision. By using the track changes feature on her computer to complete the review, the reviewer is able to visually indicate problem spots to the writer. The reviewer may offer a change or may simply highlight the problem area and attach a comment to it. Writers then have the option of accepting each suggested change one at a time or all at once and/or using the reviewer's comments to revise.

It is important that reviewers not rely on any built-in spell checking or grammar checking advice when using word processing software for peer review. Although these features can be useful tools, they are no substitute for careful reading by human eyes. Grammar and spell checkers are used best when they are used to point out potential errors that the writer then evaluates before accepting any corrections offered by the software. *There, their,* and *they're* are all correctly spelled, but deciding which one is correct to use in a particular context is something that only a human can decide. Writers and reviewers should never automatically accept any grammatical or spelling suggestions offered by spell checkers and grammar checkers. Sometimes the best thing to do is to turn these features off.

Purposes

Word processors are tools like any other writing instrument in that they can be employed for individual, collaborative, and evaluative writing. The two main features mentioned here are the track changes and comment features. Many workplace writing situations are team-oriented. This means that often several people will work as a team to put together a larger document. The process of making changes and then accepting suggested changes is ideally suited to collaborative writing when each writer is responsible for generating parts of the text. In some versions, each addition and deletion is marked within the draft so that team writers can easily distinguish individual contributions to the writing task. If this feature is not available, reviewers can change the color of their text to distinguish the additions of different authors.

For the peer review of early drafts, suggesting changes should be done less frequently than using the comment function because early drafts often need help with development and exploration of ideas. This help is often best given through comments that draw the writer's attention to strengths and weaknesses of his argument, topic, organization, and use of examples as well as the overall message of the text. These "big picture" issues need to be addressed before a fine-tuning of language and arrangement can take place. After all, most writers learn more about their topics as they write and develop their ideas in new directions.

In terms of peer review, word processors are often used to make more efficient use of time, provide an interface with which students are comfortable, and extend peer review outside of the traditional classroom. For the visual learner, embedded comments and suggestions offer an immediate visual recognition of areas that need more attention. Using word processors in this way allows students to capture peer review comments in a portable format that can be easily shared with other group members and/or members of the same class.

Advantages and Disadvantages

Using word processors to comment on drafts offers reviewers the benefit of physically locating their comments within the text in a more legible way than they could with handwritten comments in the margins of a paper. Also, word processors enable users to print copies of commented drafts for other group members and instructors to review. Track Changes in Microsoft Word is a straightforward and easy-to-use feature that does not require significant experience to be used effectively. Students can experiment with using different colors for their comments or turn the feature on and off without losing earlier comments.

One of the disadvantages of working with files rather than papers is that files can be corrupted and/or accidentally deleted. Once their feedback is lost, many reviewers feel too discouraged to repeat the peer review exercise. In addition, students have to coordinate their exchange of word-processed files to complete the review. Unless there is an established method for this exchange to take place, some students may feel intimidated by the technological knowledge required to transmit, alter, save, and return an electronic file.

Teachers often assume that younger students have strong computing skills. Students should not be afraid to let instructors know if they do not understand how to complete a computer-based exercise or assignment. If instructors do not know their students need help, then they may not explain how to save and transport electronic files, how to send files as e-mail attachments, and how to use word processing software to access and comment on those files. These are basic skills, but no one was born knowing how to do these things, and no student should be embarrassed about asking for help.

Peer Review Using Methods of Electronic Distribution

What Is It?

Discussion boards are electronic spaces, like Web sites, that enable users to post files and other information for others to see. Some look similar to online chat spaces where one user may begin a conversation on a topic that other users continue through posts that are then displayed. The string of posts that develops is called a thread. Discussion boards can have one or many threads going all at the same time. Usually one person is the owner or moderator of the discussion board and begins new threads and/or stops ongoing ones. Some discussion boards permit users to upload files attached to their posts. These files can be images, sound clips, or documents.

List serves are e-mail lists that are often used by instructors as discussion spaces. A list serve has a set number of members and may or may not be closed to members outside of the class. Individuals cannot subscribe to or send messages to closed lists without the approval of a list owner. Lists have e-mail addresses just like people and list members receive messages from other list members as e-mail messages. To send a message to a list, all one has to do is to send an e-mail to the list's address. Once sent, that message will be distributed to every member of the list.

Courseware is Web-based course management software that instructors often use to distribute information, manage grades, and communicate with students. Two of the most common kinds of courseware in use are WebCT and Blackboard. Both programs have built-in discussion boards. They also have an internal e-mail function that enables students and teachers to send e-mails to each other that may be stored as messages inside the courseware environment.

Common Practices

The mechanics of peer review via a discussion board or list serve are very similar to other methods. Once the draft has been distributed, reviewers may choose to use the track changes method and upload the draft, complete with comments, back to the list or discussion board. Or, reviewers might choose instead to read the draft online and then send one long series of comments to the author via e-mail, without making comments inside the writer's draft. The method chosen should match the stage of the writing process in which the review takes place. Early drafts often benefit more from long narrative comments that focus on "big picture" features of writing rather than short comments that focus on usage, grammar, and/or flow. Therefore, long, narrative comments sent over e-mail might be adequate for early drafts when reviewers wish to comment on main ideas, topic, and overall message of the text. Later drafts often require a finer-grained analysis that is best accompanied by in-text comments.

Sometimes instructors will create discussion boards in Blackboard and WebCT for their composition courses. If instructors allow posts to the discussion board to have attachments, then students can access other students' drafts and upload their responses.

Purposes

In recalling the five steps of any peer review from Chapter 1, notice steps two, four, and five:

1. Identify peer review partners/participants
2. Exchange drafts to be reviewed
3. List items to be targeted in the review
4. Read drafts/comment
5. Exchange reviewed drafts

Steps two, four, and five all involve the physical exchange of student work and access to that work. List serves and discussion boards do two important things for teachers and students who use them for peer review. One, they can make the physical exchange of student work quicker and easier, and extend that exchange outside of the physical classroom. Two, these electronic methods of delivery "store" the writer's draft so that it can be accessed as a file that can then be saved on a group or reviewers' hard drives.

One of the hopes of electronic peer review, in general, is that it might eliminate the awkwardness that some students feel in social group situations. For people who are shy or who feel uncomfortable talking to others about areas of a text that need improvement, electronic peer review usually makes them feel more at ease when exchanging ideas. The goal of electronic peer review is not to provide an alternative to social interaction. But, some students genuinely feel unusual stress if they have to come up with specific comments about another student's writing in one class period. For students who feel this way, much of their anxiety can be eliminated by having time outside of class to gather their thoughts and compose thoughtful responses to a student's text. There is no rule that says peer reviewers have to give instant feedback.

Advantages and Disadvantages

There are two main differences between using pen and paper for peer review and using electronic technology. First, posting papers on discussion boards or sending them out on e-mail lists enables recipients to read and respond to the drafts outside of class. This can give students more time to read and then develop thoughtful comments. It can also accommodate students whose lives require them to spend time off campus. Electronic delivery of drafts and their reviews does not require physical proximity. Writers and reviewers can post drafts and reviews at different times of the day without having to arrange for a meeting time and place.

There are disadvantages to engaging in peer review by remote access. Without the physical cues of face-to-face contact, writers are sometimes unclear about what reviewers are trying to communicate. In addition, the time delay between the posting of a draft to a discussion board or e-mail list and the reviewer's accessing of the draft can make it difficult for a reviewer to ask the writer questions and receive timely answers. Without any guidance from the writer, reviewers can put most of their time and energy into commenting on areas of the draft that are not those the writer might have thought needed the most help.

The second difference between this and the traditional method of peer review is that this method of distributing drafts can be more public than the in-class, three-person peer group. *More public* means reviewers and writers can have the opportunity to see comments of more than one peer reviewer. This can be helpful when writers are struggling with similar challenges and are able to see a variety of suggestions within a short span of time. When reviewers want suggestions for how to structure their comments, they often appreciate seeing what other reviewers have said. But, this can also become a problem if drafts and reviews contain content that unintended viewers find objectionable. Additionally, drafts containing personal stories could become public pieces that can potentially be accessed by individuals outside the class. It is usually a good idea to not post texts to the Web that contain personally identifying information. When in doubt about the public nature of any class list or discussion space, students should ask their instructors about who will have access to student posts.

Peer Review Using Web-based Peer Review Software

What Is It?

Web-based peer review software programs are available to students and their teachers, and more still are in use by professionals in a wide variety of fields. The one most commonly available to students is Exchange, which can be accessed through codes included when one purchases some new textbooks. Students begin to use Exchange by typing in the access codes provided to create user IDs and passwords.

Once they are able to log on to the peer review site, students may:

1. Upload papers for review
2. Review papers already uploaded by their peer group members
3. Read comments left for them by other reviewers
4. Read comments left by instructors
5. Send e-mail to other peer group members
6. Export reviews to their hard drive

Some instructors might use the peer review program to grade student work and post grades in an online grade book. Different programs offer different features to students and teachers, but their primary function is the same: to facilitate the exchange of written drafts between students for the purpose of peer review.

Common Practices

In many ways, conducting peer review using a program like Exchange offers students the combined best features of the previously discussed electronic peer review methods. Programs like Exchange typically facilitate the following aspects of peer review:

1. The creation of groups, either at random or as selected by the instructor.
2. The posting of documents for peer review with notification sent to group members letting them know a draft has been uploaded.
3. A reading pane for the reviewer to view the document. The pane includes easy to use buttons for comments, review questions, and contact of group members, all on one screen.
4. A list of questions, either generic as included with the software or specific as uploaded by an instructor, that students can use to complete their peer reviews.
5. The ability to stop the review and restart it at a later time without losing previously entered comments.

6. Lockouts that prevent drafts from being uploaded after the due date, thereby encouraging peer review groups to have their drafts uploaded in a timely fashion.
7. Tracking features that enable instructors to view both drafts and comments posted and also to comment on any student's draft.
8. The ability to simultaneously view all comments on a single draft left by all reviewers. Different reviewers' comments are usually in different colors.
9. The ability to save the original draft on the Web server and lock it so that reviewers' comments do not alter the original text. This also means the file cannot be lost or accidentally deleted by a reviewer.
10. Comments, as with the comment feature in Microsoft Word, can be connected to specific portions of text and common responses can be saved for reuse.

In one possible scenario, instructors using Exchange may tell students that a writing assignment is listed on Exchange and it needs to be peer reviewed before it is turned in. Students might or might not be given time in class to access and work in Exchange.

Once logged into the program, students can access the assignment and then upload their draft. Peer review group members may receive an e-mail once a fellow group member has posted a paper for review. Students engage in the review by clicking another student's draft as listed under headings like "reviews to complete." Once the draft appears on the screen, the reviewer will see other boxes surrounding the text. When he clicks on an area of the draft that needs a comment, a chat-like or instant messenger-like box appears. The reviewer can decide if a comment should be connected to a word, sentence, paragraph, or the entire draft. Once comments are entered, they become visible to the reviewer and later to the writer via a reading pane located immediately next to the original draft. Carrots (small graphic pointers) and highlighting help communicate to the student what specific areas of the text relate to the comments provided. Once a draft has been reviewed and the responses finally posted, comments cannot be edited or deleted. This preserves the original intent of the reviewer so that the writer can consider one comment at a time. Writers may be informed of a completed review via an e-mail from the peer review program.

Purposes

Web-based peer review programs, like Exchange, are often used because they provide a more structured peer review environment for students. Because these programs were designed solely for peer review, their features automatically point students toward positive and productive review activities. Students find few distractions in a peer review program environment. Unlike word processors that have been adapted to peer review, specific programs like Exchange focus exclusively on the peer review process. Every feature is intended to support the exchange and review of student drafts in group settings similar to traditional classroom-based small groups. Using programs like Exchange can be more attractive to teachers because students often seem more connected to the classroom environment than when they use stand-alone word processors or even courseware sites.

If every student is using Exchange, or another similar program, then every student is facing similar technological and procedural challenges. This makes it easier for teachers to get students on track and to focus on the peer review process. Other electronic methods can sometimes leave students feeling as if they are alone on islands, each facing unique platform and procedural challenges. If every student is using the same program, it doesn't matter who has what brand of computer or who has what approach to reading drafts. The teacher can address whatever questions come up for everyone rather than attempting to solve several different technological problems. In short, one main advantage of using a program like Exchange is that it puts the focus on the peer review process and not on the technology that enables that process.

The Web-based nature of programs like Exchange ensures that both students and teachers can access the materials. Users can access their drafts and conduct reviews from virtually any computer that is connected to the Internet.

Advantages and Disadvantages

Advantages of the online, Web-based peer review program over other electronic methods of peer review include the ability to distribute drafts, receive drafts, give comments, and receive comments using the same interface. This can save time as well as enable students to see other students' reviews if they are working in the same peer review group. Programs often allow teachers to set up groups to be assembled randomly, removing the problem of coordinating with classmates to complete reviews. Other common features include an export option that enables writers to export their drafts with comments to a separate file that they can save on their computer.

These programs, like Exchange, offer students and teachers the ability to maximize the benefits offered through electronic peer review. Using them in class offers students more time to respond to other students' drafts because it takes less time to compose and add comments. The separate comment and draft panes also solve some of the neatness issues of traditional peer review sessions. This feature eliminates both the messiness of handwriting and the sometimes overwhelming visual effects of drafts reviewed via word processors. In addition, the communication feature of programs like Exchange enables students in groups to capture some of the social interaction of traditional peer review without sacrificing the advantages offered by remote access and electronic communication.

Electronic Peer Review Group Dynamics

What Is It?

It might not seem like groups function any differently in virtual spaces than they do in real life. The reality of working in groups in virtual settings can often be more challenging than students expect. Reading and responding to classmates' written work is not quite the same kind of interaction that happens through instant messaging, e-mail, text messaging, blogging, or other kinds of electronic communication. This section will examine some of the more common challenges faced by students working in peer review groups in online spaces.

How to Select Peer Reviewers

A section in Chapter 1 talks about how to select peer review partners for traditional peer reviews in or outside of class. Electronic peer review groups should be compiled using similar criteria. If students are allowed to select their peer review groups, they need to consider the dependability, sincerity, and seriousness of potential review partners. Just because reviews are taking place on computers does not mean that the best peer review partner is going to be the biggest computer genius in the class. Technology skills are important, but groups need only be competent at using the technology required for completion of the peer review. Members should not have to be computer science geniuses to employ electronic technology for their reviews.

Dependability is more important in electronic peer review members because of the independence afforded through the use of technology in distributing drafts, posting reviews, and sharing comments. Students should seek out peer review partners who are willing to provide completed drafts as early in the process as possible, and definitely before the due date set by the instructor. If a peer group member is late in posting her draft for review, then the other group members may not have adequate time to read and respond to that draft.

In addition, some peer review programs create random groups as papers are uploaded. Some students might think that they do not have to read and respond to other papers until their paper is posted for review. To avoid negative outcomes, group members should have an understanding of when they plan on completing their reviews. Getting everything finished by the due date assigned might be fine with the teacher, but if students need more time with their responses in order to integrate them into their revisions, they need to be sure their peer review partners understand their needs and expectations. A review that arrives too late is about as useful as no review at all. Selecting the right peer review partners has everything to do with how well the group can and will work together.

Things to Remember When Responding to Writing Online

Plugged into the Internet or not, computers do change the way people respond and react to the ideas of others. One of the advantages of conducting peer review online is the time saved through typing comments rather than handwriting them. This same speed of communication can have a negative side. The slow labor of writing a response by hand gives the brain time to consider how the draft's author will receive that response. Quick comments keyed in on the computer can happen so fast that the brain doesn't always catch language that might be less than helpful, and may even be hurtful.

For example, let's say I'm reading a draft for my peer review partner about steroids. The draft's thesis might be:

> Steroids are a great way to enhance athletic performance, but only the strong will survive using them.

My immediate response to this sentence might be less than kind. I might think that it is a rather strange and goofy idea. Beyond that, I might wonder how the writer plans on supporting a thesis like this, because it seems an odd claim to try to prove. I might even wonder if I should take the writer seriously. If I begin typing my comments as soon as the thoughts pop into my head, I might say something rather mean to the writer without realizing that my response is not providing sincere or helpful feedback. In other words, if I do not force myself to slow down and think about where the writer is coming from before I try to offer a response, I will be reacting to the ideas in the draft, not the writing.

The speed with which comments can be posted on the computer can be a dangerous thing. To try to avoid unintentional negative outcomes, electronic peer reviewers should:

1. Always read the entire draft before making any comments
2. Assume that the writer is being sincere in his claims; give him the benefit of the doubt even if the ideas seem strange
3. Always re-read all comments and responses before making the review public to the writer or anyone else
4. Never, ever send a response when aggravated or angry

Negotiating and Commenting on Difficult Content

Most people who have been using e-mail as a means of correspondence have at one time or another sent a "flaming" message to someone. Those heat-of-the-moment letters are usually regretted as soon as they are sent and almost never solve any of the problems that motivated their composition in the first place. Writing when angry can be a cathartic exercise on paper, but is more likely to be disastrous online if the angry text is ever made public. Responding to fellow classmates' drafts when angry should be avoided at all costs, regardless of the situation.

As mentioned in the previous section, the efficiency of communication offered by electronic technology can make it difficult for students to remember to take their time when composing peer review responses online. Should they encounter content that seems violent, hateful, or otherwise inappropriate, the correct response is to talk to the instructor. It is not a good idea to respond by reacting to the text with offense and anger. On the flip side, students who create inappropriate texts and place them on discussion boards or course Web sites run the risk of being penalized if their behavior violates school policies. This situation can become even more serious if the posts are readable on the World Wide Web.

Students should not forget that writing can be a deeply personal thing to some people. Just because one person's ideas in a draft might seem outrageous or even impossible, that is not a reason to give a hurtful response to that draft or react negatively to the writer. Although it is true that everyone in writing classes probably needs to develop a few calluses when it comes to their feelings about their own writing, the need for a thicker skin does not justify intentionally insulting another student's work.

In the end, the best thing that online peer reviewers can remember is that their comments may be visible to others beyond their peer groups. If every comment is posted as if it could become completely public, students probably will not have to worry about offending anyone. Students who take peer review seriously, offer sincere and thoughtful comments, and provide timely feedback will most likely receive the same in return on their written drafts.

3

ADDITIONAL RESOURCES

What Is It?

Chapter 3 contains examples and additional resources for students wanting to learn more about peer review. It contains the following:

- Sample #1: a typical draft with handwritten comments
- Sample #2: an early draft with comments inserted using a word processor
- Sample #3: a developed draft with comments
- Sample #4: a revised draft after peer review using track changes to display the revisions
- A list of additional reading on writing

These samples employ the questions suggested in Chapter 1 for peer review both of an early draft and of a developed draft. Samples 2 and 3 offer some idea of what peer review using electronic technology might look like. Sample 3 is an approximation of what a peer review using typical peer review software might look like, because it is not possible to reproduce an actual peer review software interface in this book.

The sample student drafts listed in this section were taken from *Learning Together: An Introduction to Collaborative Learning*, 1st ed. by Tori Haring-Smith.

The list of additional reading includes handbooks and other practical guides for student writers. Sources listed relate to writing and/or group dynamics similar to those experienced in peer review.

Sample #1: A Typical Draft with Handwritten Comments

The following sample provides a typical, fairly successful student paper. Notice the handwritten comments and other markings on the student's text. Is this an effective method of communicating a peer response? Are this reviewer's suggestions easy to understand? Would a student want to receive feedback in this fashion?

Negligence and Inadvertence

While dealing with the issue of criminal responsibility, H. L. A. Hart comments on Dr. Turner's arguments and gives his point of view. This paper will consider the section entitled "Negligence and Inadvertence" and present its relevance to both moral and legal responsibility.

The crux of Hart's argument is centered around the definition of negligence as "a state of mind." This seems a bit harsh. Rather than claim negligence as a state of mind, inferring something that cannot be controlled, I see it as more of a conscious decision to disregard some precaution. Regardless, Hart describes its validity concerning criminal responsibility with reference to manslaughter. First of all, he works under the condition that someone can be held criminally responsible only if he had it in his mind or had an intention to cause bodily harm. This holds well, for how can someone be held responsible for someone's death if the action that caused it was involuntary? Only when the action was caused by negligence.

So a dilemma is presented: if one is criminally responsible only if bodily harm was intended, then it should follow that one is not criminally responsible if bodily harm was not intended. But this can be easily disproved. Hart uses the example of a construction worker mending a roof in a busy part of town and the debris of his work is thrown down. It is quite obvious that the worker's only intention is to complete his job in a clear area; nevertheless, if someone is walking by and is hurt by the falling material, the worker must be held responsible for the injury. Why? Because he was negligent—he failed to take any precautionary measures or even consider the consequences of material falling into a street.

Just as the worker is held criminally responsible for the consequences, he is similarly held morally responsible. Although Hart does not discuss moral implications regarding negligence, I have come to the conclusion that moral responsibility must be ascribed to one who has been negligent, even if he/she is not found criminally responsible. But this circumstance is rare, for if one is found to be criminally responsible, it is assumed that a contributing factor to this verdict is the person's failure to be morally responsible in the given situation.

While pondering the issue of moral responsibility and its relation to criminal responsibility, I became intrigued with the concept of being criminally responsible without being morally responsible. What if a robber came into a bank with the sole intent of making off with the money, and he even went so far as to bring a toy gun so that no one would be hurt? Should he be held both criminally and morally responsible for any unfavorable outcome even though he went out of his way to ensure that no one would be caused any bodily harm? The answer is yes, and implies that even with good intentions, one is held accountable for both breaking the law and causing harm.

Then there is the question of the degree of negligence required to make a person accountable (or not). Dr. Turner asserts that a concept of degrees of negligence is absurd but both Hart and I disagree with such an assertion. If we return to the example of the construction worker and examine the situation, we find there are certain levels of precautions he could have taken that would have deterred anyone from being injured. They range from the obvious (looking before throwing down debris) to the less obvious (shouting down to any pedestrians to take care, or putting up a warning sign). The less obvious the precaution is, the more thought and care was exerted in the task. Therefore, the more obvious the precaution, the more he is responsible— and blameworthy.

Blameworthy is a term that designates a definite tone concerning the responsibility of the person in question. Hart relates negligence with blameworthiness only to enforce and introduce another concept to negligence, that of inadvertence.

While the dictionary defines *inadvertence* as, "unintentional, accidental," Hart prefers to describe it as a direct translation of negligence. I strongly disagree because while negligence connotes blame or reproach, inadvertence implies blamelessness. Yet, both terms are connected by the fact that (A) harm is caused to someone or something and (B) both could have been prevented.

And prevention, or the amount of mental exertion needed to ensure that no one is harmed, is the base for a decision of criminal or moral responsibility. Returning to the issue of manslaughter, Hart feels that two questions should be asked in order to determine one's responsibility. The first is if harm was intended, and the second is if he acted in "a fit of inadvertence." But then he has contradicted himself because he previously mentioned that for criminal responsibility, mere inadvertence is not enough. Therefore, he resorts to the claim that an act of negligence is essentially the same as acting in a fit of inadvertence.

If for criminal responsibility negligence and inadvertence are alike, does the same hold for moral responsibility? If someone was harmed during the robbery where the robber had come only with a toy gun, the harm could not be attributed to negligence. The harm was not premeditated, nor was it caused by a failure to take normal precautions. It was caused by a distraction from the main event—it was caused inadvertently. Therefore, unlike negligence alone, whose implications follow both criminal and moral responsibility, negligence and inadvertence work together criminally but not morally.

There is one final point concerning negligence that Hart encounters. It deals with the act of omission. It is his opinion that negligence (being a state of mind) is the omission of precautions that are required by a certain standard. Omission in itself is a heavily discussed concept with regard to criminal and moral responsibility. Usually one is convicted due to actions that are committed, but, in a sense, the omission of an action is committing an action, just as not deciding between two choices is a decision in itself. But I regard his reference to omission as too harsh. Instead of an omission of precautions, I see it as more of a failure to take necessary precautions.

In conclusion, I agree with some general areas of Hart's arguments, but find the definitions of some terms inaccurate. The question of criminal responsibility is solved but moral responsibility is left up to the reader. It is this question of morality which will help the reader relate these theories to the "real world," giving a more universal perspective to such a narrow concept.

Sample #2: An Early Draft with Comments Inserted Using a Word Processor

This draft is typical of an early attempt to transfer ideas into a working document. As you read, notice the grammar and spelling errors. These are not uncommon at this stage because the writer is working out ideas, not formulating the final text for her assignment. Reviewers should not spend their time correcting these types of errors. Notice the lack of organization in this text. This student would have benefited from creating an outline before putting the draft together. Several comments target this lack of organization. Notice that the final comment offers some suggestions for improving this organization in the writer's next revision.

> **"** *This thesis sentence seems too informal. Some of its language might antagonize rather than entice readers. As a main idea, this sentence might be difficult to support since it is based on personal opinion.* **"**

Advertisements of today do not shape modern values as much as advertising analists claim they do. From the standpoint of the viewer, I consider advertising of today to be designed only for the unstable, insecure and extremely gullable person as well as the uneducated child. Only being one of these types of people, could I agree with advertising analysts.

How can any average, knowledgeable, basically secure individual be swayed, in establishing his or her values, by the advertisements of today? They merely insult human intellect by being set up for the IQ of a three or four year old. The developers design their advertisements for emotional appeal, popular appeal (the "in" things), and snob appeal. They are only failing when they do this because the average person sees right through

> **"** *I cannot locate the main idea of this paragraph. The idea that "seeing through advertisements makes viewers immune to them" seems like an interesting idea to develop further as a main point for this paragraph, but it will need support through either examples or outside source material.* **"**

the advertisement. That is, in consciously knowing what the developer is trying to accomplish in his advertisement he becomes unmoved by the purpose of it.

If a person were unstable, insecure and very gullable advertisements could play an important part on the origin of their values. Because he is unstable, emotional advertisement appeal could move him in decisions. Being insecure would influence his attitude toward advertisements of popular and snob appeal. Also, if he is gullable enough to not see through them he could easily be influenced by them.

> 66 *This main idea fits with your thesis, but it is unclear and needs more support. It might be improved with clearer language that explains how "unstable," "insecure," and "gullible," are being defined for the purposes of this paper.* 99

Children of little formal education are probably most influenced by advertising. Saturday morning television is filled with advertising for children. Obviously the exciting new tops that "Tommy" or "Susi" have are ideally what the child wants. At that age he is striving to be accepted by as many other youngsters as possible. By having those toys He is now more like them. Aksi he has the attitude that "Tommy's" parents got him this toy and I can have it too?" Advertisements make the child expect these things otherwise he may psychologically think his parents don't care about his wants. He may even think they don't love

> 66 *This paragraph does a good job of expressing a main point and supporting it through explanation. It might function even better if the first sentence is revised to explain how "formal education" fits. The logic of how this paragraph appears here instead of earlier or later is not clear. A more obvious sense of organization would be helpful.* 99

him as much as "Tommy's" parents because of the great emphasis placed on having these toys through advertising.

Values and attitudes of today are shaped mostly by individual or group experiences among piers, family and friends

> **"** *The idea expressed in the first sentence of the paragraph is interesting, but it seems disconnected from the thesis. The thesis needs to be revised to incorporate these ideas or this paragraph might not fit with the rest of the paper.* **"**

of the opposite sex. Actual everyday occurrences, contacts, and conversation mold the values of persons today. These person to person relationships have much more of a dynamic influence on ones attitudes, values etc. Because of close ties among certain individuals, there is more influential contact also. This type of value and attitude shaping is also one the intellectual level of that specific individual or group of individuals.

> **"** *The idea connecting advertising influence to the shaping of people's values is interesting. But, if this is one of your main points, it does not come through in this paper. Perhaps you might try looking for outside sources that study advertising's effect on people to see if there is one aspect you might focus on. Your example of advertising that targets children is well done and might be a good idea to expand into an entire paper. As this stands now, (it is not clear which issue you wish to focus on (connecting advertising to belief formation, advertising targeting children, advertising encouraging snobbery). Any of these issues are interesting, but this might seem like a clearer paper if you just picked one to focus on.* **"**

Sample #3: A Developed Draft with Comments

This example attempts to represent the viewing pane of peer review software programs like Exchange. It is not a perfect rendition because there are more ways that the program indicates connections between comments and the text.

Alcohol is a generalized central nervous system depressant. As such, its effect is to depress the centers of the brain that mediate inhibitions, judgment, and control. Individual neurons become less excitable, repolarize more slowly after excitation, and exhibit reduced spontaneous electrical activity. Synaptic nerve transmission is impaired. Spinal reflexes are depressed. In addition, neuromuscular coordination (speech, gait, manual dexterity) is reduced, as in visual acuity, and perception of pain and fatigue. <u>Why then, does a little drinking so often seem to have a stimulating effect?</u>

> " *This seems like the thesis for this paper. It is a good organizing idea, but some people might be put off by it being phrased as a question.* "

In the past, alcohol had been thought of as a uniformly depressant drug. <u>Excited speech and behavior occurring after a little drinking had been attributed to the aforementioned depressant effects of alcohol on the mechanisms that normally regulate these activities.</u> Although this may be true, this was widely accepted as the <u>total</u> explanation. It is now recognized that alcohol, ultimately a depressant, does indeed first act as a stimulant.

> " *This sentence is confusing. I think I know what you are trying to say, but it could probably be broken up into two separate sentences for clarity.* "

<u>The first action of alcohol on neural tissue is to irritate, agitate, or stimulate. Although spinal reflexes become depressed as intoxication increases, they are initially enhanced. Responses to the irritant effect of alcohol can be observed in the gastrointestinal tract. The nausea that can occur after the use of alcohol probably stems from gastrointestinal inflammation. Diarrhea may be provoked by the irritant properties of various oils present in most alcoholic beverages</u>.

> " *This paragraph is well written and interesting, but it is not clear how it fits with the thesis or the other main points. Perhaps a more obvious connection between "irritation" and "stimulant" would help.* "

The concept of alcohol as a stimulant has been further demonstrated in an <u>experiment</u> where intelligent subjects

> **"** *The experiment described is good support for the thesis of this paper, but, the source of this information needs to be appropriately documented in either MLA or APA format. A sample problem would add further support.* **"**

> **"** *This example does support the main idea of the paragraph and does make connections to the thesis, but, it needs to be cited and/or the source of the information needs to be documented for it to be credible.* **"**

were given small doses of alcohol (2–4 ounces whiskey). They were required to solve highly demanding intellectual problems such as Boolean logic. It was found that their performance after ingesting a small amount of whiskey was superior to their performance when sober or following the ingestion of larger amounts of whiskey.

Finally, there may be more mundane reasons for the apparent stimulation observed after a little drinking. The calories from the alcohol provide a "quick energy boost." In social situations someone may just feel "high" or happy the minute a drink is in their hand. It may be a signal that it is time to party. There would be an initial stimulation until the depressant effects set in. So, alcohol can be seen initially as a stimulant having both physiological and psychological manifestations. Yet the ultimate effect of alcohol in high doses is always as a depressant. The euphoria and excitement that one derives from drinking, with increased intoxication, leads to confusion, stupor, coma, and perhaps death.

Sample #4: A Revised Developed Draft After Peer Review Using Track Changes

When English instructors talk about revision, they usually mean a substantial redevelopment of a particular paper topic or thesis. Sometimes this might mean selecting one original, but minor point, and developing it into a fleshed-out idea. The more detailed a paper is, the narrower the topic can be.

The following developed draft could have been substantially revised to focus on a variety of ideas related to, but not the same as, its original thesis—"Why then, does a little drinking so often seem to have a stimulating effect?" The following example suggests one way this paper could have been edited to clarify the original thesis instead of branching off into a new direction. The track changes feature has been used both to illustrate what it might look like and to clearly indicate what changes to the original draft have been made.

Alcohol is a generalized central nervous system depressant. As such, its effect is to depress the centers of the brain that mediate inhibitions, judgment, and control. Individual neurons become less excitable, repolarize more slowly after excitation, and exhibit reduced spontaneous electrical activity. Synaptic nerve transmission is impaired. Spinal reflexes are depressed. In addition, neuromuscular coordination (speech, gait, manual dexterity) is reduced, as in visual acuity, and perception of pain and fatigue. Despite these facts, a little drinking often seems to have a stimulating effect.

In the past, alcohol had been thought of as a uniformly depressant drug. Excited speech and behavior occurring after a little drinking had been attributed to the aforementioned depressant effects of alcohol on the mechanisms that normally regulate these activities. Although this may be true, this was widely accepted as the *total* explanation. It is now recognized that alcohol, ultimately a depressant, does indeed first act as a stimulant.

The role of alcohol as a stimulant is supported through some of the ways the body responds. The first action of alcohol on neural tissue is to irritate, agitate, or stimulate. Although spinal reflexes become depressed as intoxication increases, they are initially enhanced. Proof of the irritant effect of alcohol can be observed in the gastrointestinal tract. The nausea that can occur after the use of alcohol probably stems from gastrointestinal inflammation. These reactions are ways that the body can respond to stimulants.

The concept of alcohol as a stimulant has been further demonstrated in an experiment where intelligent subjects were given small doses of alcohol (2-4 ounces whiskey) (Smith 304). The subjects were required to solve highly demanding intellectual problems such as Boolean logic. It was found that their performance after ingesting a small amount of whiskey was superior to their performance when sober or following the ingestion of larger amounts of whiskey (Smith 306).

Finally, there may be other reasons for the apparent stimulation observed after a little drinking. The calories from the alcohol provide a "quick energy boost." In social situations someone may just feel "high" or happy the minute a drink is in their hand; It may be a signal that it is time to relax and have fun. There would be an initial stimulation until the depressant effects set in.

Alcohol can be seen initially as a stimulant having both physiological and psychological manifestations. Yet the ultimate effect of alcohol in high doses is always as a depressant. The euphoria and excitement that one derives from a little drinking, diminishes with increased intoxication, that can lead to confusion, stupor, coma, and perhaps death.

Additional Reading on Writing and Peer Review

Here are some additional resources for students wanting to know more about the writing process and about the aspects of group dynamics functioning in team writing and peer review.

Anson, Chris M., and Robert A. Schwegler. *The Longman Handbook for Writers and Readers (with MyCompLab)*. 4th ed. New York: Longman. 2005.

Barnet, Sylvan, Pat Bellanca, and Marcia Stubbs. *A Short Guide to College Writing (Penguin Academics Series), A.* 2nd ed. New York: Longman. 2005.

Brown, John Seely, and Paul Duguid. *The Social Life of Information.* Harvard Business School Press. 2000.

Bruffee, Kenneth A. *Collaborative Learning: Higher Education, Interdependence, and the Authority of Knowledge.* Baltimore: Johns Hopkins University Press. 1999.

Faigley, Lester. *The Penguin Handbook.* 2nd ed. Longman. 2006.

Fowler, H. Ramsey, and Jane E. Aaron. *The Little, Brown Handbook.* 10th ed. New York: Longman. 2007.

Haring-Smith, Tori. *Learning Together: An Introduction to Collaborative Learning.* 1st ed. New York: Addison-Wesley. 1993.

Kolln, Martha J. *A Rhetorical Grammar: Grammatical Choices, Rhetorical Effects.* 5th ed. New York: Longman. 2007.

Stewart, Greg L., Charles C. Manz, and Henry P. Sims. *Team Work and Group Dynamics.* New York: Wiley. 1998.

Veit, Richard, and Christopher Gould. *Writing, Reading, and Research.* 7th ed. New York: Longman. 2007.

Williams, Joseph M. *Style: The Basics of Clarity and Grace.* 2nd ed. New York: Longman. 2006.